SOME MAJOR EVENTS IN WORLD WAR II

THE EUROPEAN THEATER

1939 SEPTEMBER—Germany invades Poland; Great Britain, France, Australia, & New Zealand declare war on Germany; Battle of the Atlantic begins. NOVEMBER—Russia invades Finland.

1940 APRIL—Germany invades Denmark & Norway. MAY—Germany invades Belgium, Luxembourg, & The Netherlands; British forces retreat to Dunkirk and escape to England. JUNE—Italy declares war on Britain & France; France surrenders to Germany. JULY—Battle of Britain begins. SEPTEMBER—Italy invades Egypt; Germany, Italy, & Japan form the Axis countries. OCTOBER—Italy invades Greece. NOVEMBER—Battle of Britain over. DECEMBER—Britain attacks Italy in North Africa.

1941 JANUARY—Allies take Tobruk. FEBRUARY—Rommel arrives at Tripoli. APRIL—Germany invades Greece & Yugoslavia. JUNE—Allies are in Syria; Germany invades Russia. JULY—Russia joins Allies. AUGUST—Germans capture Kiev. OCTOBER—Germany reaches Moscow. DECEMBER—Germans retreat from Moscow; Japan attacks Pearl Harbor; United States enters war against Axis nations.

1942 MAY—first British bomber attack on Cologne. JUNE—Germans take Tobruk. SEPTEMBER—Battle of Stalingrad begins. OCTOBER—Battle of El Alamein begins. NOVEMBER—Allies recapture Tobruk; Russians counterattack at Stalingrad.

1943 JANUARY—Allies take Tripoli. FEBRUARY—German troops at Stalingrad surrender. APRIL—revolt of Warsaw Ghetto Jews begins. MAY—German and Italian resistance in North Africa is over; their troops surrender in Tunisia; Warsaw Ghetto revolt is put down by Germany. JULY—allies invade Sicily; Mussolini put in prison. SEPTEMBER—Allies land in Italy; Italians surrender; Germans occupy Rome; Mussolini rescued by Germany. OCTOBER—Allies capture Naples; Italy declares war on Germany. NOVEMBER—Russians recapture Kiev.

1944 JANUARY—Allies land at Anzio. JUNE—Rome falls to Allies; Allies land in Normandy (D-Day). JULY—assassination attempt on Hitler fails. AUGUST—Allies land in southern France. SEPTEMBER—Brussels freed. OCTOBER—Athens liberated. DECEMBER—Battle of the Bulge.

1945 JANUARY—Russians free Warsaw. FEBRUARY—Dresden bombed. APRIL—Americans take B[...]sen and Buchenwald concentration cam[...] Russians free Vienna; Russians take over Ber[...] Mussolini killed; Hitler commits suici[...] MAY—Germany surrenders; Goering captured.

THE PACIFIC THEATER

1940 SEPTEMBER—Japan joins Axis nations G[...] many & Italy.

1941 APRIL—Russia & Japan sign neutrality pa[...] DECEMBER—Japanese launch attacks against Pe[...] Harbor, Hong Kong, the Philippines, & Mala[...] United States and Allied nations declare war [...] Japan; China declares war on Japan, Germany, Italy; Japan takes over Guam, Wake Island, Hong Kong; Japan attacks Burma.

1942 JANUARY—Japan takes over Manila; Jap[...] invades Dutch East Indies. FEBRUARY—Japan tak[...] over Singapore; Battle of the Java Sea. APRI[...] Japanese overrun Bataan. MAY—Japan takes Ma[...] dalay; Allied forces in Philippines surrender to Ja[...] an; Japan takes Corregidor; Battle of the Coral S[...] JUNE—Battle of Midway; Japan occupies Aleuti[...] Islands. AUGUST—United States invades Guad[...] canal in the Solomon Islands.

1943 FEBRUARY—Guadalcanal taken by U.[...] Marines. MARCH—Japanese begin to retreat [...] China. APRIL—Yamamoto shot down by U.S. A[...] Force. MAY—U.S. troops take Aleutian Islands ba[...] from Japan. JUNE—Allied troops land in N[...] Guinea. NOVEMBER—U.S. Marines invade Bo[...] gainville & Tarawa.

1944 FEBRUARY—Truk liberated. JUNE—Saipan [...] tacked by United States. JULY—battle for Gua[...] begins. OCTOBER—U.S. troops invade Philippin[...] Battle of Leyte Gulf won by Allies.

1945 JANUARY—Luzon taken; Burma Road w[...] back. MARCH—Iwo Jima freed. APRIL—Okinawa [...] tacked by U.S. troops; President Franklin Roosev[...] dies; Harry S. Truman becomes preside[...] JUNE—United States takes Okinawa. A[...] GUST—atomic bomb dropped on Hiroshima; Russ[...] declares war on Japan; atomic bomb dropped [...] Nagasaki. SEPTEMBER—Japan surrenders.

WORLD AT WAR

Mussolini:
A Dictator Dies

WORLD AT WAR

Mussolini: A Dictator Dies

By G.C. Skipper

 CHILDRENS PRESS, CHICAGO

The hotel in the Gran Sasso Mountains of the Appenines where
Benito Mussolini was held captive by the new Italian government

FRONTISPIECE:
Mussolini smiles at the camera during a
1939 tour of northern Italy.

Library of Congress Cataloging in Publication Data
Skipper, G   C
   Mussolini, a dictator dies.

   (His World at war)
   SUMMARY: Details the last days of the man who
founded Fascism and ruled as dictator of Italy for
almost 21 years.
   1. Mussolini, Benito, 1883-1945—Death and burial
—Juvenile literature. 2. Italy—History—German
occupation, 1943-1945—Jvenile literature. 3. Heads
of state—Italy—Biography—Juvenile literature.
[1. Mussolini, Benito, 1883-1945—Death and burial.
2. Italy—History—German occupation, 1943-1945.
3. Heads of state] I. Title. II. Series.
DG575.M8S54   945.091'092'4 [B] [92] 80-25345
ISBN 0-516-04790-6

Copyright© 1981 Regensteiner Publishing Enterprises, Inc.
All rights reserved. Published simultaneously in Canada.
Printed in the United States of America.
   2 3 4 5 6 7 8 9 10 R 83 82 81

PICTURE CREDITS:
UPI: Cover, pages 4, 6, 9 (left, top and
bottom), 10 (top), 12, 13, 14, 15, 16, 18,
19, 20, 21, 22, 26, 27, 29, 30, 32, 35, 36,
37, 38, 41, 42, 45, 46
U.S. ARMY PHOTOGRAPH: pages 9 (right),
10 (bottom)
LEN MEENTS: page 25 (map)

COVER PHOTO:
Mussolini inspecting members of the
Italian Legion after they had returned
from fighting with the Nationalists in
Spain

The hotel was high in the Apennine Mountains in central Italy. The day was September 12, 1943. World War II had been raging for four years. Over most of the world, the Allied nations were battling against the threat of Nazi Germany, Fascist Italy, and the rest of the Axis nations.

Adolf Hitler was the leader of Nazi Germany and the leader of all the Axis nations. His close friend was Benito Mussolini, called *Il Duce* (the leader). Mussolini was the leader of Fascist Italy.

At the hotel on that September day the war seemed far away. The mountains that would soon blaze with autumn colors seemed peaceful. But this was not the case. Around the small, isolated hotel stood armed Italian guards. They seemed unaware of the beautiful mountains. Their main concern was the man they were guarding.

Under arrest, on the second floor of the hotel, was Benito Mussolini. This was the same man who had been the feared dictator of Fascist Italy for nearly nineteen years. He was the same man who was Hitler's close friend and ally.

Two months earlier, the Fascist Grand Council had met. Rebels in the group had voted to remove Il Duce from power. The government would be returned to King Victor Emmanuel III.

Things had gone very badly for Benito Mussolini. As he stared gloomily out of the hotel window, bitter memories came to him. His own son-in-law and foreign minister, Count Galeazzo Ciano, had been one of those who had voted against him. Mussolini remembered the indignity of his arrest. He had been shipped off to jail in an ambulance—on the very day the king had regained power!

The people had not lifted a hand to help him. They remained silent. He had been shuttled from one place to another until, finally, he had been brought to this place. The small hotel was isolated, high in the mountains.

Above: Marshal Pietro Badoglio, the premier of the new Italian government. Behind him is a portrait of King Victor Emmanuel.
Left: Happy Italians cheered in the streets and threw rotten vegetables at a Mussolini poster when they learned he had been taken out of office.

In July 1943, Mussolini had been stunned to learn that the Allies had invaded Sicily and that his Italian troops there had given up.
Top: Troops aboard a transport plane hear that they will be the first Americans to land in Sicily. Bottom: Troops landing on the beaches of Sicily.

Mussolini had heard he was to be turned over to the Allies. In July the Americans had landed in Sicily. That had done it, Mussolini had thought at the time. The Italian army had collapsed. They had gone down like cardboard soldiers. But the worst news had come only a few days ago. On September 3, the Allies had landed in Italy itself. And only five days after that came the final blow. The government that had replaced Mussolini had surrendered to the Allies. Surrendered!

Now the sun was coming in through the hotel window. Mussolini stared out. His bald head caught the light. Suddenly his eyes narrowed. His eyebrows went up in surprise. A huge grin spread across his face.

As he watched, a glider had appeared. Then another one. Without engines, the gliders sailed quietly across the sky. They circled slowly down toward the hotel.

Germans! Mussolini thought. Hitler has come to rescue me!

German paratroopers, led by the legendary commando Otto Skorzeny, scale the mountainside to reach the hotel and rescue Benito Mussolini.

Down below, the Italian guards continued to pace. Suddenly one stopped dead in his tracks.

"Look!" he shouted to his companion. "Nazis!" Then the gliders were down. Nazi troops jumped out. They quickly overwhelmed the guards. The other Italians saw what was taking place. They turned and ran toward the safety of the mountains.

Not a single shot was fired. The Nazis moved in and hauled Mussolini out.

Above: Mussolini stands in front of the hotel with his rescuers. The man with the mustache, second from the right, is Skorzeny.
Below: The paratroopers give a Nazi salute as Mussolini is led off to the small Fieseler Storch plane that will fly him out of the mountains.

They put him in a plane that had landed in a nearby meadow. They took him straight to Adolf Hitler.

After Hitler and Mussolini had been reunited, Hitler spoke firmly to the Italian dictator. Hitler let it be known that he was not pleased with Mussolini's Italian army. He wanted Mussolini to return to Italy and establish a new Fascist government.

During the "March on Rome" in October 1922, Italian Fascists burn Socialist literature in the streets. Shortly afterward, because the Fascist Party founded by Mussolini had become so strong, King Victor Emmanuel III made Mussolini prime minister. Mussolini stayed in power from that time until his downfall and arrest in July 1943. Now, after his rescue, Hitler wanted him to return to Italy and form a new Fascist government.

Hitler and other Nazi officals greet Mussolini on his arrival in Germany.

Mussolini was so depressed, however, that he barely heard Hitler's words. When they were through talking, Mussolini requested notes from the meeting. Then he returned to Italy. But he did not return to Rome. That would have been too dangerous. Instead, he set up his new government on beautiful Lake Garda, near the town of Gargnano in northern Italy.

Mussolini tried to regain his old high spirits and drive. He recalled that Hitler had once told him that both of them were called by history to greatness.

Yet, nothing seemed to help. Mussolini knew he

Count Galeazzo Ciano, Italy's foreign minister (above), was married to Mussolini's daughter Edda (right). Ciano was executed in 1944 for his part in the July 1943 overthrow of Il Duce.

was only Hitler's puppet. Nazi Germany yanked the strings and Fascist Italy jumped.

This was proved dramatically in November 1943. Hitler insisted that Ciano—Mussolini's son-in-law—be arrested. After all, Ciano had helped to remove Mussolini from power. Hitler wanted him punished. He wanted him executed.

The pressure was too great for Mussolini to withstand. He finally yielded to Hitler's wishes. He ordered Ciano's arrest and execution. In January 1944 Ciano was shot, along with other Fascist leaders who had been involved in the overthrow of Il Duce.

Mussolini continued to go through the motions of running a Fascist government. But he knew it meant nothing. His country was in turmoil. In October 1943 Italy had declared war on Germany. Italian partisans joined the Allies to stop Hitler. The partisans hated Fascism. They wanted their country to be free of German domination. They fought against the Germans who were still in Italy. They fought against their fellow Italians who still followed Mussolini. There was street fighting all over Italy.

Mussolini knew the Axis nations were on the verge of losing the war. It was simply a matter of time—and not very much time. Mussolini felt as if he were tied to a drowning man. There was nothing he could do to keep from going under with Hitler.

By the spring of 1945, Mussolini's worst fears had been realized. The Allies had crossed the Po River on their way north. The Italian partisans had taken control of many Italian cities and towns.

Mussolini went through the motions of running a Fascist government,
but he never regained his old spirit. Above: He reviews troops.
Below left: He discusses the disastrous military situation in
Italy with Field Marshal Erwin Rommel and German ambassador Rahn
in February 1944. Below right: Hitler greets Mussolini on his
arrival in Germany on June 10, 1944. This meeting took place
only four days after the Allies had invaded Normandy on D-Day
and six days after Rome had fallen. Time was running out for both men.

Above: Thin and weak, Mussolini reviews Fascist troops in Milan.
Below: American troops on their drive into Rome in June 1944.

Mussolini knew that time had run out. He was no longer safe where he was. He left for the town of Como, in northwest Italy. Como is at the foot of the Alps, not far from the Swiss border. Before he had been there long, however, Mussolini realized he would not be able to stay. To avoid capture and execution, he would have to cross the border into Switzerland. There, he might have a chance.

On April 26, 1945, dawn broke in a drizzling rain. Mussolini and a small group took off in the

The Villa Deste, near Como, where Mussolini stayed for a while after fleeing from his Lake Garda villa, which was no longer safe.

This 1938 picture shows Mrs. Mussolini (left) and her two youngest children (foreground). The three did not make their escape into Switzerland after all, but were caught at the border on May 2, 1945.

rain. They drove along the winding roads near the shore of Lake Como.

As the car sped along, Mussolini watched the rain trickle down the windshield. He wondered whether his wife and children would make it to Switzerland. Surely they would. He had said good-bye to his wife in a dark, rain-soaked garden in Como. There he had given her papers. He had told her, "If they try to stop you or harm you, ask to be turned over to the English."

Mussolini shook his head. No sense dwelling on that, he thought. Surely the family will get through. After all, there were letters signed by Winston Churchill in those papers.

Clara Petacci, Mussolini's girlfriend, traveled with the group trying to escape to Switzerland.

"Will the Black Shirts follow us?" Mussolini suddenly asked. The Black Shirts were Italian soldiers loyal to him.

"Yes, Your Excellency," replied one of his companions. "Pavolini is bringing them."

"And there will be 3,000 Black Shirts?" asked Mussolini.

"Just as you ordered, Your Excellency."

"Good, good!" replied Il Duce. He suddenly seemed to cheer up. His mind turned to other matters, more pleasant ones. With him, traveling in another car with her brother and his family, was Mussolini's girlfriend, Clara Petacci. He smiled, thinking of her.

"Is there someplace we can rest?" asked Mussolini after awhile.

"Yes, Your Excellency. Not far ahead is Menaggio. There is a local Fascist official who will welcome us."

Mussolini nodded in agreement. Not long afterward the group pulled up and stopped at the official's house. Mussolini went inside and slept.

Hours later he awoke to a great noise. Outside he could hear the grinding of gears and the revving of engines. Hurriedly he got dressed and went outside. There, strung up and down the highway, he saw a large convoy—loyal followers, including Germans, who had followed him.

"Get those vehicles out of sight!" Mussolini ordered.

"Yes, Your Excellency!" one of the soldiers replied, alarmed.

Mussolini stormed back into the house. "We have to leave immediately. It is too risky to have all those vehicles lined up out there!"

While the convoy was being moved into side roads and, hopefully, out of sight, Mussolini's small party took off again.

The word soon spread that Il Duce was gone. The big convoy cranked up again and followed him.

Mussolini, along with Clara, finally arrived at the Hotel Miravalle. Hot on their heels came the convoy. Soon, the entire group was at the hotel.

Mussolini went inside and stayed there. His men needed rest. Besides, the entire countryside was crawling with partisans.

"Has Pavolini arrived with the Black Shirts?" Mussolini demanded.

"Not yet, Your Excellency."

"We might as well wait here until dawn," Mussolini said.

During the night, Pavolini finally arrived. Mussolini rushed out to greet him—only to learn that the 3,000 Black Shirts were not with him.

"How many do you have?" demanded Mussolini.

Pavolini looked embarrassed. He swallowed and then said, "A dozen, Your Excellency. But they are the best fighters of all of them!"

In happier days for Mussolini, he had thousands of followers (above). By the time of his escape attempt, only twelve Italian Black Shirts joined him.

"Twelve!" shouted Mussolini. "Only twelve! Where are the others?"

Pavolini looked very uncomfortable. He swallowed again. "They surrendered, Your Excellency."

Mussolini said nothing more. He glared at Pavolini. Then his face seemed to sadden behind the firm stare. "Tomorrow at dawn we leave for Switzerland," he said. Then he went back into the hotel.

For years, Mussolini addressed Fascist crowds from the balcony of his Pallazo Venezia (left). After Rome fell, the building across from the famous balcony became the Rome headquarters of the Allied Command (right).

The countryside was swarming with partisans. Mussolini was now riding in the car with Clara. He looked anxiously out the window. The convoy moved along the roads. Soon it passed through the village of Musso.

"What time is it?" Mussolini asked.

"Six-thirty," Clara told him. "We'll reach Switzerland before long. You'll see." She squeezed his hand. Il Duce turned his face back toward the car window.

Suddenly, as they left Musso, the harsh explosion of gunfire blasted the air. The convoy halted immediately.

"What's the problem?" asked Mussolini.

Outside he could hear the Germans in his convoy talking loudly, yelling back and forth.

"There's a huge tree across the road!" one of them shouted.

"It's a partisan roadblock," called another.

Ahead of them, the Germans escorting Mussolini could see the large tree sprawled across the road. Barbed wire covered it.

An old man had been walking slowly along the side of the road. When the warning blast was fired by the partisans, the old man had stopped. He looked anxiously at the convoy. Suddenly a gun barked again. It came from the convoy. The shot was meant for the partisans who had thrown up the roadblock. But it accidentally struck the old man. He dropped instantly, dead.

"Don't be an idiot!" someone in the convoy shouted. Immediately another soldier in Mussolini's convoy raised a white flag. They did not want any trouble or any more shooting—not with Mussolini riding back there in the car.

The partisans cautiously approached the convoy. They were armed with pistols and rifles. "Where do you think you're going?" one of the partisans asked.

This troopship on the way to the Italian colonies in Africa in 1935 was strung with warlike photos of dictator Benito Mussolini.

Mussolini was photographed with many Nazi officials over the years. The German Fascists, not the Italians, were his friends at the end. Here he is shown with Adolf Hitler (top left); Wilhelm Keitel (top right); Hermann Goering (bottom left); and again with Adolf Hitler (bottom right).

"We are Germans," replied one of the men with Mussolini. "We are going toward Austria to help the German army. We have no argument with Italians."

"Our orders are to stop anyone who tries to get through here," replied the partisan who seemed to be the leader.

"We have an agreement with the partisans to pass through," replied the German. He had no such agreement. But neither did the partisans have orders to halt the convoy. The two parties stared at each other. For a long time, nothing happened. The convoy sat still. The partisans refused to let them go any further.

"All right!" the partisan leader finally said. He knew he could not stall the convoy much longer. "All Germans will be allowed to pass. However, the Italians who are traveling with you must be turned over to us."

"We can't do that!" replied the German. "We have our orders!"

"You have no choice," replied the partisan leader.

While the Germans huddled to decide what they should do, a voice suddenly shouted, "Bellini! Come here, Bellini!"

The partisan leader turned and saw one of his men trotting toward him. Bellini shouldered his rifle and walked toward the man. When the two met they were out of earshot of the convoy.

"What's the problem?" Bellini asked.

In 1904, Mussolini (top left) was a revolutionary in Italy. Later, as *Il Duce*, he had a statue made that showed him as a Roman emperor (left). The kitchen in the home where Mussolini grew up (top right) was in great contrast to his luxurious sitting room in the Pallazo Venezia (above).

"Mussolini is with the convoy!" the partisan said. He was very excited.

"That's impossible!" Bellini replied. This could not be true, he thought.

"I tell you, it's true!"

"Very well. I'll check it out." Bellini motioned for one of his officers. "Now get back to your post," Bellini told the partisan.

As the partisan ran off, the officer came up to Bellini. "Yes sir?" he asked.

"We have a rumor that Mussolini himself is with this convoy. Check it out." Bellini said.

"Yes sir!" answered the officer. But when Bellini turned to go back to the waiting Germans, the officer grinned to himelf. "Some time for a joke!" he said aloud. He turned and went on about his business. After all, Bellini couldn't be serious.

A settlement was finally reached. Bellini agreed to let the convoy go one mile farther, to a town called Dongo. One civilian car would also be permitted to proceed to Dongo. This was the car in which Clara rode with her brother, who was posing as a Spanish consul.

Although Bellini did not know it, while the Germans were stalling, they had whisked Mussolini out of Clara's car. They had dressed him in a German army overcoat and helmet. Mussolini had then taken a place in one of the open trucks.

The convoy moved off. Mussolini was riding in the open truck. At Dongo, however, they were stopped again. This time the partisans began checking papers. They checked all the papers—including those of the Germans who were riding in the open truck.

During the check, one of the partisan inspectors came running to the partisan leader, Lazzaro.

"Mussolini is in that truck back there!" he said urgently.

"What?"

"I recognized him, Lazzaro! I saw him with my own eyes. Mussolini is here!"

During his days in power, Mussolini rode in style in an
open limosine with Nazi official Rudolf Hess. Now he had
to ride in an open truck disguised as a German soldier.

"Let's take a look," Lazzaro said.

The two partisans walked back to the truck.
Lazzaro walked up to the man in the overcoat
and helmet. "Camerata!" he said, tapping the
man on the shoulder.

"Leave him alone," one of the German soldiers
said. "He's drunk."

Lazzaro once more tapped the man's shoulder.
"Excellenza!" he said. The man did nothing.
Lazzaro persisted, crying out, "Cavaliere Benito
Mussolini!"

The man moved slightly then. Lazzarro wasted
no more time. He leaped up on the truck and
walked to the man. Lazzaro reached down and
pulled off the man's German helmet. The man

sat. He was wearing sunglasses. The collar of the
overcoat was turned up around his ears. Lazzaro
reached down and removed the man's sunglasses.
Then he flipped down the collar of the overcoat.

Lazzaro could not believe his eyes. Here, in
front of him, holding a machine pistol, sat
Benito Mussolini. The feared Duce of Italy!

"Do you have any more weapons?" Lazzaro
asked.

Without speaking, Mussolini unbuttoned his
overcoat. He gave the partisan leader a long-
barreled 9-mm Glisenti automatic. He does not

The photos on these pages show
Mussolini as he liked to be thought
of—a proud, manly sportsman and
pilot. By the time of his arrest
by the partisans, Mussolini was
a different man—worn out and old.

look frightened, Lazzaro suddenly thought. He
looks worn out and old.

Lazzarro took a deep breath. Then he said, "In
the name of the Italian people, I arrest you!"

By now a crowd had gathered around the
truck. They shouted out angrily as Mussolini got
to his feet. "I won't do anything," Mussolini
said.

"I promise you safety," Lazzaro answered.
The crowd yelled loudly. Noisy threats were
shouted as Lazzaro led Mussolini through the
mob toward the town hall.

It did not take long for the partisans to discover that the papers of the Spanish consul were fake. They promptly arrested both Clara and her brother.

By sundown that day, the partisans had agreed that Mussolini had to be moved to a safer place. If he weren't, the crowd outside would kill him.

The partisans and Mussolini took off in an open car. The plans were to take him to the barracks at Germansino. Then they would whisk him away to a secret place that would be safer.

The joy shown by these Italian civilians when they heard that Mussolini had left the country for a trip to Germany in 1944 was only a small indication of the joy and relief they felt when they learned of his capture by Italian partisans in 1945.

"Tell Clara not to worry about me," Mussolini told the partisans. They agreed to deliver his message.

Clara, much to the surprise of the partisans, wanted to be with Mussolini—no matter what. She said, "You must promise that if Mussolini is shot, I can be near him until the last moment and that I shall be shot with him. Is that too much to ask?"

It was a hard decision to make, but finally the partisans agreed to grant Clara her request.

That night it was raining very hard. The partisans took Mussolini from the barracks. They placed a bandage around his head so he would not be recognized, and took off for the secret hiding place. As the car in which they were riding turned a curve in the road, it came upon another car parked by a bridge.

"You may ride in the other car," Mussolini was told. "Clara is in that car waiting for you."

The dictator again got out into the heavy downpour. He ran to the other car.

The partisans had planned to take the prisoners to Como. But as they neared the town, they learned that the Allies were rounding up all Fascists. The partisans changed their minds. They turned the car back and drove in the hard rain for a few miles. When they reached a small town, they left the car and began walking.

Sloshing through the mud, they walked through the town. They continued walking out into the fields, toward a neighboring village.

There, in the first house they came to, they hid Mussolini and Clara.

Meanwhile, word of Mussolini's capture had reached partisan headquarters in Milan. This was to mean the end for Il Duce. Immediately, officials at Milan sent a man named Walter Audisio to get Mussolini. His orders were simple. He was to shoot Mussolini and Clara when he found them.

These Italian patriots were part of the group sent
from partisan headquarters in Milan to execute Mussolini.

The following day, April 28, 1945, Audisio took
off with fifteen armed partisans. At Como,
however, other partisans stopped them. But not for
long. Audisio, who used the name Colonel
Valerio while fighting with the partisans, yanked
out a pistol. He demanded that his fellow
partisans call Milan to check his story.

Finally, at one-thirty in the afternoon,
Colonel Valerio reached Dongo. He demanded
that Mussolini and Clara be turned over to him.

The lives of Adolf Hitler and Benito Mussolini, the two Fascist leaders pictured on this 1941 stamp, came to an end within two days of each other.

By four o'clock Valerio was at the farmhouse where Mussolini and Clara were hiding. He pounded on the door. When it opened, he rushed upstairs and into the bedroom. He cried, "I have come to rescue you!"

Mussolini looked at the man as if he were crazy. But all Il Duce said, in a tired, sarcastic voice, was, "Really?"

Mussolini and Clara were hurried out of the house and into a car. They had traveled only a short distance when the car came to an abrupt halt. It stopped in front of a large iron gate. Beyond the gate was a villa.

"What's the problem now?" Mussolini asked.

"I heard a noise," Valerio replied. "I'm going ahead to see."

He jumped from the car and ran off down the road.

He was not gone very long. Soon he came back and called out softly, "Hide near the gate! Be quick about it!"

Mussolini and Clara got out of the car and hurried toward the iron gate.

Then, without any other warning, Colonel Valerio shouted, "By order of the general headquarters of the Volunteers for Freedom Corps I am required to render justice to the Italian people!"

"No, he mustn't die!" Clara screamed. She threw her arm around Mussolini's neck. "He musn't die!"

"Get out of the way!" Valerio shouted. "Move or be shot!"

Clara stepped aside, terrified. Valerio straightened and aimed his pistol at Mussolini. He pulled the trigger.

The gun jammed. It did not fire. Angered, he threw down the pistol and grabbed another one. It, too, jammed and wouldn't fire.

Valerio finally got his hands on a third gun. When he did, he aimed it at Mussolini and shot him five times. The gun jerked in his hand, spitting sparks that paled in the sunlight.

Clara watched in horror as Mussolini fell forward. Then Valerio turned the gun on her. Clara's request was about to be granted. She was shot with Mussolini and died with him.

Early the next morning—Sunday, April 29—the bodies of Mussolini and Clara were hauled back to Milan and dumped in the town square. The Milanese people went insane when they saw the dictator they so despised. The angry mob attacked the bodies, kicking them and mutilating them. At last the mob spent its anger and began to drift away. The bodies of Il Duce and his Clara were strung up by their feet in the square—for all to see and for all to remember.

The bodies of Fascist Party secretary Achille Starace, Benito Mussolini, and Clara Petacci (left to right) were strung up by their feet in the Milan town square after their execution by Milanese Italian partisans.

This huge portrait of Mussolini, which had once hung
in a place of honor in Fascist headquarters in Anzio,
Italy, became a target for passing Allied soldiers.

INDEX

*Page numbers in boldface type
indicate illustrations*

About the Author

A native of Alabama, G.C. Skipper has traveled throughout the world, including Jamaica, Haiti, India, Argentina, the Bahamas, and Mexico. He has written several other children's books as well as an adult novel. Mr. Skipper has also published numerous articles in national magazines. He is now working on his second adult novel. Mr. Skipper and his family live in North Wales, Pennsylvania, a suburb of Philadelphia.